Sewing
Accessories

A Collector's Guide

Sewing
Accessories

A Collector's Guide

Elaine Gaussen

MILLER'S SEWING ACCESSORIES: A COLLECTOR'S GUIDE
by Elaine Gaussen

First published in Great Britain in 2001 by Miller's, a division of
Mitchell Beazley, imprints of Octopus Publishing Group Ltd,
2–4 Heron Quays, London E14 4JP

Miller's is a registered trademark of Octopus Publishing Group Ltd

Commissioning Editor **Anna Sanderson**
Deputy Art Director **Vivienne Brar**
Senior Art Editor **Rhonda Fisher**
Project Editor **Emily Anderson**
Designer **Louise Griffiths**
Editor **Mary Scott**
Proofreader **Miranda Stonor**
Indexer **Sue Farr**
Picture Research **Nick Wheldon**
Production **Catherine Lay**
Jacket photography by **Steve Tanner**

ISBN 1 84000 353 7
A CIP catalogue record for this book is available from the British Library
Set in Bembo, Frutiger and Shannon
Produced by Toppan Printing Co., (HK) Ltd.
Printed and bound in China

Jacket illustrations, front cover, left to right: Mother-of-pearl reel
holder, c.1820, £20–35/$30–55; Scissors in silver-plated sheath, c.1850,
£55–95/$90–150; Card needle packet holder with portrait of Byron,
c.1870, £40–55/$65–90; Velvet and silver plate pin container, 1860–80,
£14–20/$22–30; Royal Doulton Glass thimble, c.1980, £5–15/$8–25;
back cover, above: Ornate brass pen knife, 1860–70, £15–35/$25–55;
below: Small silver button hook for a chatelaine, c.1820, £15–20/$25–30;
half-title page: French opaline etui, c.1865, £750–900/$1,200–1,450;
contents page: English needle and pin holder, c.1870, £50–65/$80–105

contents

Introduction

Sewing accessories have been around from the time people first began to dress in clothes, and have been positively traced to the 15th millennium BC with the finding of palaeolithic bodkins in riverside caves in southern France. The first thimbles may have developed with the discovery of bronze around 3,000 BC. Byzantine thimbles from the 9thC to 12thC AD were discovered in Corinth, and the earliest thimbles found in Britain are also from around this time.

It is generally only possible to date sewing accessories by century or period. The 18thC and 19thC were the heyday of creativity with a needle. The most decorative and intricate tools were made in Paris during the 19thC and are now identified by the term "Palais Royal".

Sewing accessories generally include all tools made to assist a seamstress or embroideress. However, the boundaries of this collecting hobby are blurred as they can extend to include tools for making lace, fine decorative netting, crochet and knitting. Not surprisingly, examples of the needlework that was made using these sewing accessories attract attention in their own right, and are often an accepted part of a collection.

It is not only the tools and accessories themselves that draw many to this absorbing hobby. The design and function of tools shed light on the fashions of a period, as well as the social history of the time, as sewing accessories were used across all stratas of society. Tools of a more utilitarian quality were used by the poor as they worked in dim light in cottage industries, making garments and household linens for sale. The more decorative tools were used by ladies' maids in large houses, for repairs and alterations and for making household linen. Exquisite, highly decorative and sometimes less functional sewing accessories were used by wealthy ladies. Occasionally a young lady would receive an etui (an ornamental container with miniature tools) upon reaching a standard of excellence in needlework.

Although much has been written about needlework, the subject of sewing accessories received little attention until the late 19thC, when the first publication on the subject was issued by a French author. This was followed in 1928 by Gertrude Whiting's *Tools and Toys of Stitchery*, reprinted in 1971 under the title *Old-Time Tools and Toys of Needlework*. The book created considerable interest in the subject, initially in the USA. In 1966 the enthusiasm for sewing accessories spread to the UK when Sylvia Groves wrote *The History of Needlework Tools and Accessories*, which took research into a new dimension. Since the 1970s more collectors have conducted research and shared their findings, often through member societies, and an extensive interest in these functional, beautiful and delicate tools has developed.

Below left: advertising tape measure, c.1930, **£5–15/$8–25**; below right: cardboard advertising pincushion, c.1920, **£5–8/$8–13**

Collectors are sometimes dismayed to find that their descendants do not wish to inherit their prized collection, which has been carefully compiled over many years. In such circumstances it is better that the tools are sold at auction, giving others a chance to buy and treasure them. Some collections have, of course, been given to museums, but before embarking on that course of action potential donors need to be aware that the accessories would probably not be on show for much of the time; those who wish to view at museums know this only too well, as they are usually required to arrange the visit in advance.

One of the greatest benefits of collecting sewing accessories is the number of permanent friendships that arise out of it, each person widening the knowledge and experience of the other. Among the unexplained mysteries between collectors are why so many never actually come to use a thimble, despite their keen interest in the subject, and why so many are, or have been, nurses.

Included in the book are just some of the sewing accessories that absorb a large and ever-growing group of collectors who share a fascinating hobby that will last a lifetime.

Above: reproduction of an early needle pusher, length 2.5cm (1in), **£5–8/$8–13**

Prices & dimensions

Prices vary depending on the condition of the item, its rarity and where it is purchased, so the prices given are an approximate guide only. The sterling/dollar conversion has been made at a rate of £1 = $1.60. Dimensions, where given, are to the nearest half centimetre/quarter inch and refer to the figure illustrated. The abbreviation L to R is used for left to right.

Collecting advice

Collectors of sewing accessories are passionate in their search for the elusive and may, in the course of their hunt for these pieces, gather an international network of friends with whom they can share information. There are member societies to join (see pp.60–61) and it can be especially useful to view antique tools in museums and at auctions and fairs.

What to collect

The range of sewing accessories is extensive and there are varieties within categories, each of which can form an interesting collection. Thimbles, for example, are a suitable category for creating sub-divisions. Take time to formulate a collecting strategy: many new collectors are attracted to a wide range of sewing accessories and collect indiscriminately. Before long, purchases exceed display space and among the good pieces are some of little interest, which have limited resale potential.

L to R: Torville & Dean thimble, **£2–5/$3–8**; witches' coven thimble, **£5–10/$8–16**

Reproduction of an ancient thimble, **£1.50–3/$2.50–5**

Display

When embarking upon collecting, consider the space available to display the pieces. Does your home lend itself to extending the collection beyond one wall or room? Displaying 500 thimbles will require several frames, and a modest collection of general sewing tools can fill a number of cabinets. Accessories should be kept under glass, free from dust and away from the eye of casual callers.

Condition

Purists only collect items in perfect condition. This is a slow process, but the resale potential is normally good. A rare item that is slightly imperfect may be the only one of its type that the collector will come across. If a better version appears in the future, the option is there to resell in order to buy better.

Cost differentials

Collect for enjoyment: financial gain should be regarded as a bonus. Market trends are variable year on year, between countries and even between cities and provincial towns. What is rare and costly in one country may not be so

in another. This particularly applies to price variations between the UK and the USA. Expect higher prices in large towns, cities and major fairs, although such locations also offer the opportunity to buy from experienced specialist dealers who travel extensively to find the best pieces. Alternatively, the collector who is prepared to get up early and travel to country fairs and auctions may find lower prices but, in real terms, the one balances out the other. Christies in South Kensington, London, and Phillips of Solihull in the Midlands hold specialist auctions of sewing tools to which collectors travel from all over the world. Prices are high, with many wanting the same pieces. Collections from the USA now frequently come under the hammer at these venues. Catalogues, together with prices realised, give an indication of trends and can become collectable in their own right. View before bidding, establish the condition of the piece and set your maximum bid. Something special may be found amongst a lot, but not identified in the catalogue. Always try to be present at the sale and stick to your bid. There are often others prepared to go to financial heights to secure what they want. Commercial clubs and mail-order dealers operate internationally and issue sales catalogues, web sites and lists. Member societies usually include buying and selling sections in their newsletters. Collectors are entitled to add a figure to the original purchase price to reflect inflation when selling to their peers. Nonetheless, the absence of overheads often makes this a reasonable way of buying.

Gimmicks, reproductions & fakes

Some modern sewing accessories, although made and marketed "For Collectors", are not worthy of inclusion in a collection. However, if they are clearly marked as reproductions, some of these items can be an alternative to the collector who does not have the financial resources to purchase the genuine article.

However, reproductions purporting to be the real thing must be avoided. They are usually of inferior quality with, where applicable, a poorly cast hallmark. A thorough knowledge of sewing tools will help to avoid such pitfalls.

Bog oak pincushion, 1930s, **£30–45/$50–70**

Small thimble display case, **£1.50–5/$2.50–8**

Containers

In the reigns of William IV (1830–37) and Queen Victoria (1837–1901) ladies carried sewing accessories when they travelled, so miniatures were crucial. These could be stored in various containers: an etui, a small, frequently decorative container, held tools in its frame and tools were also suspended from the waistband by a chatelaine. Some household staff used chatelaines – the more tools, the higher their rank – but the lady of the house would possess an elaborate version. Then came sewing purses – small bags containing fitted tools and a piece of needlework. Finally, a hussif was a tiny cylindrical sewing set, with a thimble as the lid and sometimes a seal on the base. Originating in 17thC Germany, it typically held needles, pins, threads and, frequently, collapsible scissors.

◄ Hussifs
The term hussif is derived from the German word for housewife and describes various small sewing sets. The design was adapted in Europe and the USA and manufactured in the early 20thC. It was particularly popular in the Art Nouveau and Deco periods. The hussifs shown are both German: the brass example would have been fixed to a waistband and holds a penknife, needles, pins and bodkins; the lid of both hussifs is a thimble.

L to R: brass hussif, 1860–70, **£30–60/$50–95**; enamel hussif, 1890–1910, **£90–140/$145–225**

▲ Etuis
Etuis were usually given to reward excellence in needle-work. By pressing down on the top shell of this example, the egg opens to reveal a platform holding a selection of small useable tools: a thimble, a perfume bottle, a bodkin, a stiletto, a pair of scissors and a needlecase.

French mother-of-pearl and gilded brass egg etui, on a marble base, c.1870, **£150–250/ $240–400**

English steel chatelaine, c.1880,
£125–250/$200–400

▶ **Steel chatelaines**
Invented in the 12th–13thC,
a chatelaine was the insignia
of the mistress of a castle,
from which the French name
is derived. It was suspended
from the waistband by a
clasp. Chains attached to the
clasp held many different
kinds of accessories, but
few carried more than
the sewing chatelaine,
first thought to have
been popular in the
mid-17thC. In the
18thC the central
chain often carried
a complete etui.
Chatelaines
underwent a
revival in the late 19thC. This
faceted steel chatelaine carries
(left to right) a propelling
pencil, pincushion, scissors,
penknife, thimble and wind-
up tape measure.

English leather chatelaine, 1900,
£100–300/$160–480

Working chatelaines
Working chatelaines
were worn by ladies
with responsibility,
either in managing a
wealthy household or
in a profession such
as nursing or teaching.
Other types of chatelaines
were made, some carrying
single items such as a pair
of spectacles in a case, a
fob watch or a spool
knave. There were also
multi-functional versions
that carried a number
of different tools.

▼ **Utility chatelaines**
Utility chatelaines were the
tools of office for housewives
in the late 19thC. Many have
perished – hence the high
price of those that still survive.
The leather chatelaine
illustrated holds (left to right)
a pincushion, needles in a
purse, a notebook and pencil
(which recorded a proposed
visit to "Miss James,
St Thomas' Hospital – 3pm")
and scissors in a sheath. The
owner and "Miss James" may
well have been nurses, as
many wore such
chatelaines
around 1880
to 1910.

▼ Sewing purses

With the revival of chatelaines at the end of the 19thC came an interest in other ways of carrying sewing implements. Sewing purses were often less expensive than chatelaines and therefore were more widely affordable. Relatively small, the purses often held a surprising number of tools that were not always miniatures, unlike those commonly found in etuis. The purse shown below measures 8.5 x 7.5cm (3¼ x 3in) and contains a useable thimble, scissors, needlecase, stiletto and tambour with four interchangeable hooks, plus two packets of needles, embroidery thread and a small piece of embroidery from the late 19thC period.

▶ Nanny brooches

A "badge of office" from c.1895 was the nanny brooch, reputedly worn by nannies, though not exclusively so, in the late Victorian and Edwardian eras. They functioned as both brooches and needlecases, with the backing brass cylinder, located behind the central stone, holding needles, pins and thread for emergency repairs. The stone in most brooches was a resin goldstone – oval, oblong, round or square in shape. Other examples had glass, moonstone or expensive cameos at their centre, sometimes framed by several gilded insects.

English nanny brooch, c.1900,
£60–75/$95–120

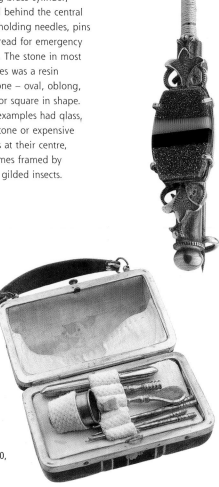

English sewing purse, c.1870,
£80–95/$130–150

Antique needlework boxes

Most antique needle-work boxes seen today date from the 19thC. They fetch high prices when in good condition. Collectors must ascertain whether the hinges, lining paper, fabric and tools are original, if any, or at least in keeping with the period, and that the wood is not warped, nor the veneer lifting. Rarely are such boxes found complete with a key to lock them. When a key is present, the box often costs a little more.

English leather sewing set, c.1900, **£25–45/$40–70**

▲ **Sewing sets**

Sewing sets appeared in number in the Art Nouveau and Art Deco periods. Parisian examples, with decorative cases and sometimes "Palais Royal" mother-of-pearl tools, are earlier. Initially the tools were stored in recessed compartments, but by 1920 each was retained by a fabric brace, later replaced with elastic. The set illustrated includes steel scissors and a silver thimble; the remaining tools are mother-of-pearl. It is an example of individual replacement having occurred: only the nail file is "Palais Royal". The case measures 11 x 14cm (4¼ x 5½in).

▶ **Needlework boxes**

Admired as objects of fine workmanship for centuries, needlework boxes were a major topic of conversation among 19thC ladies. Most came with a matching set of tools, elaborate linings, maybe a secret drawer (as shown) and some incorporated toiletries and/or writing utensils. The box illustrated, right, has an engraved cartouche that indicates that it was presented in 1876 by inmates of a workhouse to a charity worker who was leaving. She must have been highly regarded to receive a box of such quality.

English needlework box lined in classic Victorian purple, 1876, **£225–350/$360–560**

Storing & using thread

Until the 19thC thread was hand-spun and sold in skeins. The purchaser had to wind the thread, which was fragile, easily tangled and required careful storage. Card was then replaced by spindles, onto which thread was wound, housed in a cotton barrel that had a hole in the side through which the thread passed. Matching reels of ivory, mother-of-pearl, bone or wood were stored in workboxes. In the 19thC these reels were adapted to accommodate commercially produced thread. Cotton-reel trees were made from brass, base metal and wood. Produced from the mid–19th to early 20thC, they held multiple cotton reels and many had a pincushion on top. Skeins of silk were wound onto flat winders of varying designs and materials, occasionally confused with game counters.

▶ **Cotton-reel boxes**

In the early days of mechanization, thread was expensive and thus was often stored in a designated box. The cotton industry was not slow to meet this demand, and principal factories commissioned boxes in which multiple reels were sold. This photographic Mauchline-ware box was commissioned by J. & P. Coats Ltd. The picture on the lid is entitled "Crossing the River", and inside the lid is a photograph of their Fergulsie factory, which produced "Six-Cord Cotton for Machine and Hand Sewing". It holds sixteen of their reels from the period.

Mauchline cotton-reel box, c.1900, **£40–70/$65–110**

▼ **Thread holders**

"Ounce" was a white sewing thread that was first introduced into Britain from Holland in the late 18thC. It was mainly manufactured in Scotland. The English treen reel, shown below left, measures 6 x 8.5cm (2½ x 3¼in) and was used for holding handmade, skeined thread – in this instance crewel wool. The smaller Tunbridge reel was for thread of a finer, more delicate texture. Tunbridge stickware needlework boxes were traditionally fitted with at least two such matching reels.

L to R: treen reel, 1890s, **£10–15/ $16–24**; cardboard reel, 1870, **£5–8/$8–13**; Tunbridge reel holder, c.1840, **£60–120/$95–190**

▼ Stands

Cotton-reel stands are sometimes the sole subject of a collection, there being a large variety from the late 19thC to the early 20thC. Perhaps the best known and most sought after are the ornate Victorian brass stands holding 12 reels, such as the example illustrated, which stands 35cm (13¾in tall), and the tapering brass cotton-reel trees, holding 18 reels of diminishing size. They were often intended for display only, despite some being highly practical. Others were made of mahogany, iron or steel.

English cotton-reel stand, c.1870, **£125–200/$200–320**

Top: Asian cotton barrel, c.1890, **£25–35/$40–55**; bottom: Indian ivory cotton barrel, 1880, **£30–45/$50–70**

▲ Barrels

Barrels held the thread on a central spindle and were found in late 18thC and 19thC workboxes. Bone and ivory examples were imported into Britain from the East, sometimes in workboxes. Cantonese and Indian intricately carved barrels often had a knob on top that, by tightening, trapped the end of the thread, thus holding it firm. It is not easy to find matching sets. Collectors tend to buy them individually in the hope of achieving a set over a period of years.

Cotton bobbins

Large wooden bobbins that once held cotton and fine wool for weaving in the mills of Victorian Britain have today been adapted for other uses, such as trees to display thimbles or hold cotton reels. Factory workers often fashioned them into cotton-bobbin dolls, with carved heads and pliable arms. These dolls make a charming addition to a collection.

▼ American thread holders

These early 20thC silver cotton holders from the USA are functional, attractive and highly collectable. Some were ornate; others, like the one illustrated, were plain, often with initials engraved on them – in this case "EG". A tiny hole where the lid joins the base allows the thread to pass through.

Silver cotton-thread holder, 1920s, **£50–85/$80–135**

L to R: English vegetable ivory waxer, c.1865, **£35–55/$55–90**; Tunbridge stickware waxer, 1840–80, **£45–70/$70–110**

▲ Waxers

In the 18thC and 19thC, before cotton was mercerized, wax was used to help thread slide through fabric and prevent it tangling when in use. White wax or beeswax was kept in a waxer, which usually comprised two flat discs divided by a central post. These unscrewed to insert the replacement wax. The thread was run across the wax to coat it. Illustrated are two waxer/pincushion combination tools, one of Tunbridge stickware, standing 4cm (1½in) tall and the other, of vegetable ivory (corozo nut), measuring 3cm (1¼in) in height.

▼ Needle threaders

The needle threaders most commonly found today are 20thC pieces, and were often advertising "give-aways", such as on the thimble/threader combination shown here. More complex named examples include the brass "Blindfold" threader and the plastic "Witch", also illustrated, although they were perhaps not as efficient as the combination thimble design, which is still manufactured.

Clockwise from top left: "Blindfold" threader, 1940s, **£3–8/$5–13**; advertising thimble/ threader, 1925, **£8–15/$13–24**; "Witch" threader (with box), 1950s, **£1–4/$1.50–6.50**

Spool knaves

Some spool knaves were designed specifically for use in hand knitting – providing free-running yarn for the knitter, who frequently walked around as she created a garment, and preventing the yarn from falling to the ground. For knaves used in tatting and tambouring, the reel was usually of wood, ivory or steel; those for wool were of sturdy wire, with a hook to secure the yarn.

English spool knave, c.1860,
9 x 19.5cm/3½ x 7¾in,
£60–95/$95–150

▲ **Spool knaves**

In the 18thC thread was hand-wound onto a core and reels were heavier and larger than they are today. Convenience was addressed with the introduction of spool knaves, which were suspended from the waistband. The knave supplied continuous thread to a tambour hook, tatting shuttle or lace pillow. Early examples were ornate and usually made of silver. A revival in these crafts in the late 19thC saw knaves back in fashion but of simpler design, as in the example shown here, which is made of steel and silver plate.

▶ **Thread winders**

The thread winder was a convenient 19thC tool for securing lengths of skeined silk and cotton – a forerunner of the bobbins used today in embroidery and Fair Isle knitting. The larger winders were for wool. Game counters are frequently sold as winders. Cardboard, treen, glass and, in the USA, silver (see above right) were used to make winders. Versions in Tunbridge ware, bone, ivory and mother-of-pearl originally came in matching sets.

Above: American silver thread winder, c.1890, width 3cm/1¼in, **£45–140/$70–225**; right: mother-of-pearl thread winder, c.1860, width 3.5cm/1½in, **£25–50/$40–80**

Commemoratives & advertising

The most collectable antique is the commemorative, particularly a royal souvenir. The first royal wedding commemorative, recording the marriage of Queen Catherine to Charles II in 1662, was a silver thimble. Commemoratives grew in popularity as methods of communication improved. Sewing accessories issued as mementoes of coronations, royal births, weddings and jubilees in Queen Victoria's reign are highly prized today. Modern, good-quality commemoratives will most likely be valuable in time. Advertising slogans appear on some sewing tools, such as aluminium and plastic thimbles, which were given as "freebies" and sometimes in lieu of small change. A silver thimble with "James Walker Wishes You Luck" was given by a London jeweller to a bride when her groom purchased a wedding ring, and to other selected customers.

L to R: Diamond Jubilee thimble, 1897, **£250–400/$400–640**; Channel Tunnel thimble, 1994, **£30–35/$50–55**

▼ **Commemorative thimbles**

A collection of sewing accessories can comprise commemoratives alone, such is the volume that exists. Thimbles of base metal, brass, silver, gold and enamel have recorded historical events for over 300 years. Two examples from different centuries are shown here. In the 19thC such thimbles were relatively inexpensive and well used, but not so today and bidding at auctions can be intense.

▼ **Commemorative Queen Victoria needlecase**

This example is made of card, with the larger needles on the inside front and back covers, displayed against a background of yellow wild silk. Facing them are paper containers, with flaps holding the smaller needles. Around the edge of these four pages, handwritten in gold, are the significant dates in Victoria's life. The centre spread carries photographs of the Queen.

Commemorative Queen Victoria needlecase, 1884, **£80–120/$130–190**

Above: brass thimble, 1930, **£12–28/$19–45**; below: plastic thimble, 1980s, **£2–5/$3–8**

▲ Advertising thimbles

Several collectors set out some years ago to record every advertising thimble made and they have not yet finished. The English brass thimble shown above advertised "C.W.S. Tea". Many brass thimbles carried German slogans and a few were in French. The plastic thimble is an advertising medium used effectively by many collectors, primarily American, as here, in place of a business or visiting card. To be collectable (that is, worth £8–12/$13–19), aluminium examples should have an undamaged, coloured border.

▼ Advertising pinboxes & pin packets

More widely available in the USA than in Britain were the cardboard boxes in which pins were sometimes sold. They frequently carried advertising slogans. This cube, made for Pratt & Farmer Co. of New York, features 200 coloured glass-headed pins arranged in a pattern. Such boxes were also produced by Alfred Shrimpton & Sons, in Redditch, England, and by others. Pins have been used for centuries but only became inexpensive from the mid-19thC, and in the late 19thC they were still being carefully packaged. Abel Morrall, an English maker, is famous for his glass-headed (mul)berry pins which were sold in packets of 12–18. The pins were sandwiched in black paper and rolled up within a covering that advertised them, as shown.

Left: American cube pinbox, 1930s, **£15–25/$24–40**; above: English Berry pin packet, c.1920, **£3–8/$5–13**

Needlecases & pin holders

Mechanization in the mid-18thC reduced the price of needles, which up until then were purchased singly. They were sold in a variety of containers, from advertising wrappers to expensive cases. At home, wrapped needles would have been transferred to needlecases. Primitive, handmade pins of thorn or bone were used to join animal skins together to make clothing in prehistoric times. From the Roman period, bronze pins had monetary value and were used as change. In the reign of Charles I (1625–49), pins were purchased by gentlemen as love tokens. The origin of the term "pin money" came from the detailed recording of the annual household budget allocated for pins. Glass-headed pins in small packets from the 19thC, predominantly made by Kearby Beard and Abel Morrall, are collectable.

L to R: Avery scallop shell needlecase, c.1871, **£85–120/ $135–190;** Avery quadruple golden casket needlecase, c.1868, **£50–80/ $80–130**

▼ **Brass needlecases**
Both these examples are by W. Avery & Son, Redditch, England. The shell case is in two parts, joined at the base and apex, which slide aside to reveal needle compartments. The golden casket has a lifting lid, with a lever on either side sliding to raise each of four needle compartments. Both cases are marked for needles from sizes six to nine. Avery's made twenty-nine named figural cases.

▶ **Stanhope "peeps"**
These are named after the politician and inventor Lord Charles Stanhope (1753–1816), who invented a microscopic lens the size of a pinhead. In 1859, French businessman Réne Dagron was granted a patent for microfilm. He brought both techniques together to miniaturize photographs, the images being included in souvenir ware. The photographs are often thought to be postcards, but those arrived later (1884 in Europe; 1894 in Britain). This needle-case in the shape of a French parasol, its tip still intact, has a "peep" in the handle entitled "A Memory of York", which shows six views of the Minster.

Stanhope needlecase, 1860s, **£50–85/$80–135**

L to R: English ivory and vegetable ivory Stanhope needlecase with tape measure, c.1865, **£50–80/ $80–130**; Cantonese ivory needlecase, c.1880, **£35–50/$55–80**; French mother-of-pearl needlecase, c.1885, **£100–200/$160–320**

▶ **Ivory & mother-of-pearl needlecases**
Many accessories are found minus their peeps. Peeps are fragile and need careful handling to prevent images breaking up. This combination needlecase/tape measure (left) contains "A Memory of Weymouth" peep, with six views. Peeps could show as many as 16 images, or sometimes only one; they depicted portraits as well as views. The Cantonese needlecase shown is carved with tiny houses, people and foliage. The screw threads on such cases are prone to wear. The rare mother-of-pearl French parasol needlecase shown has a brass ferrule and an eagle's head handle.

▶ **Carved needlecases**
The Tyrol in Austria has a reputation for hand-carved souvenirs. This tiny rosewood needlecase, with even the squirrel's claws defined, has had some wear. The other piece, which originated in either France or Germany, is made of coquilla nut, a South American palm, and its beautiful carving is reflected in the price. A retriever rests on the top; beneath, a child plays amongst trees with its mother; below, a gentleman removes his hat to greet a lady and on the base is a carved rose. It measures 8cm (3¼in).

Left: "Squirrel" needlecase, c.1890, **£75–85/ $120–135**

Right: coquilla nut needle-case, 1830, **£140–300/ $225–480**

▼ Beadwork

Beadwork was a popular technique in both the Victorian and Edwardian eras. In addition to beaded bags, purses, belts and appliquéd decorations, beads were used to fashion a number of sewing accessories, particularly thimble holders and needle-cases. The needlecase shown below has a base of horn, over which thousands of tiny, multi-coloured threaded beads form a pattern. Collectors frequently come across these accessories in less than perfect condition. Look carefully – if even one or two beads are missing then don't buy it, as more beads will inevitably come away as the threading deteriorates.

English
beadwork
needlecase,
c.1910,
**£50–85/
$80–135**

▼ Glass

You would scarcely imagine glass to be robust enough to be used to make a needlecase, but the resourceful Victorians made them in the mid-19thC. The variety produced was small, which suggests that the makers may have been concerned about the durability of the material. The milk glass of this needlecase is supported by a thin cardboard shell, and the decoration was hand-painted when the case was complete. Not surprisingly, few have survived. The joining cylinder is a particularly vulnerable section: just one accident and the piece is lost for ever.

English glass
needlecase,
c.1850,
**£80–110/
$130–175**

▼ Enamel

There is no more beautiful enamelling technique than that created by Russian goldsmith Peter Carl Fabergé. Close on his heels were the Norwegian enamellers, principally David Andersen, who worked in the late 19thC and drew inspiration from St Petersburg. Particularly famed for his silhouette work, Andersen strove to keep ahead of competitors. The delicate guilloched back-ground of this needlecase by Andersen represents the Aurora Borealis (northern lights). The silhouette work depicts a young girl herding geese, with the tree in the distance extending into the top section of the case.

Norwegian
silhouette
enamel
needlecase,
c.1890,
**£150–275/
$240–440**

L to R: English Bilston enamel bodkin case, c.1850, **£200–350/ $320–560**; English silver filigree and brass bodkin case (with bodkin), 1750–1800, **£75–100/$120–160**

▶ **Bodkin cases**
Before buttons, hooks and eyes and patent fasteners, garments were held together with ribbon. The channels through which the ribbon (and elastic) ran were narrow, and the bodkin, the forerunner of the needle though thicker and blunter, threaded it through. Bodkins were housed in their own slender cases, which resemble long needlecases. Cases made from Bilston enamel, produced in south Staffordshire, are highly prized. The Victoria & Albert Museum in London has a large collection. The bodkin case above left is late Bilston. An earlier example would be a combination, with needle-case, bodkin case and thimble. Also shown, above right, is an English case of silver gilt filigree over brass, possibly taken from an original Chinese design.

▶ **Silver & gold**
The two needlecases illustrated right are both French. Silver figural needlecases now fetch high prices in the auction room as collectors like to find a male and female example – often a vain search. This example of a French courtier of the period stands at 6cm (2¼in). Similar cases were also made in the late 19thC of figures in contemporary costume. The 15-carat gold needlecase, far right, is beautiful in its simplicity. Measuring 7 x 0.5cm (2¾ x ¼in), this needlecase may originally have been part of a boxed sewing set.

Figural needlecases
Figural needlecases, whether in silver, metal, wood or vegetable ivory, are much prized by collectors because of the attention to detail achieved by intricate and skilled craftsmanship – usually reflected in the high prices. Even the tiniest faces show a range of expressions and emotions. The style of the garments, hats, shoes and hair of the figures is a valuable source of social history.

Left: French silver figural needlecase, 1750–1800, **£200–250/ $320–400**

Right: French gold needle-case, c.1880, **£75–110/ $120–175**

▼ Needle books

The Canton province of southern China produced much exquisite, intricate engraving in the 19thC, an example of which is shown in the needle book illustrated below, with its floral decoration back and front. Inside are two sections, each in blue silk, that hold a packet of needles. The leather case shown right has four sections for needle packets. On the outside are four needle-box prints, probably done by the artist, Baxter. Le Blond and other lithographers also made these prints to go on needle and pinboxes, which are now collected along with other sewing accessories.

Below: Chinese mother-of-pearl needlecase, 1860–90, **£60–80/ $95–130**; right: leather needlebox print needle packet, c.1850, **£45–75/$70–120**

English needle and pin holder, c.1870, **£50–65/$80–105**

▲ Pin holders

Some of the most appealing accessories were inexpensive to produce. This cardboard box has a pale green silk pincushion, with a paper bouquet captioned "To One I Love" on the lid. The outside of the box is decorated with bright mosaic paper. Inside the lid is a drawing of workers in a "Needle Stamping and Eyeing Hall", with the section beneath holding 25 steel pins. The raised centre holds four packets each containing a dozen Dorcas Needles. Victorian pictures of young girls feature on either side and the foreground flap has a mirror in it. The box was patented by W. Vale & Sons.

L to R: Flora Macdonald needle
packet, c.1920; egg-eyed needle
darners, c.1900; Hall's nickle-
plated betweens needles, c.1920;
elliptic sharps needles, c.1900;
50p–£2.50/80c–$4 (each)

▲ **Packets**
The name Flora Macdonald
is synonymous with quality
needles, which are very collectable. The Studley needle darners
have egg-shaped eyes – less
traumatic on fabric and thread
than round eyes. Betweens
needles are short and fine.
"Gold Eyd Elliptic Sharps" have
very fine points and are longer
than betweens. Needle eyes were
gold-plated to indicate quality.
As a result of vastly improved
production methods, needles
and pins from the 19thC are
now proportionately devalued.
They are usually displayed in
their package by collectors, but
glass-headed pins often decorate
pincushions of the same period.

▼ **Emery cushions**
Emery cushions were used to
burnish needles, making them
shiny and easy to slip through
fabric. The emery granules
were tightly packed to make
a hard cushion. The tool
pictured below left is an
English vegetable ivory
combination emery cushion,
pincushion and tape. Vegetable
ivory, the nut kernel of the
corozo palm, was readily turned
on a lathe. When freshly picked,
the kernel is an ivory shade,
but it darkens over the years.
The emery on the right is in a
stand of Tunbridge stickware.

Left: vegetable ivory emery,
tape and pincushion, 1860,
£45–70/$70–110; below:
Tunbridge stickware emery,
c.1840, **£45–85/$70–135**

Tusks & shells

Ivory was used to make many sewing accessories in the 19thC and was mainly taken from elephant tusks. It was turned and hand-carved, particularly in Canton, India and Dieppe in France. Ivory is difficult to differentiate from bone when carved, and only experience equips collectors to know which they are handling. Tortoiseshell comes from the shell of the hawksbill turtle and was hand-carved or engraved. Used extensively in the 18thC, frequently for veneering, it was often inlaid with mother-of-pearl or silver. Mother-of-pearl comes from the smooth, lustrous lining found in the shells of pearl oysters, abalones and mussels. It was used in the 18thC to make sewing accessories, but survival of such pieces in good order is comparatively rare because of their fragility. Mother-of-pearl was also used as an inlay in workboxes.

▶ Cases

This netting case, larger than but frequently mistaken for a bodkin case, is an example of the cases hand-carved in China for the European market in the 19thC. First practised in the 16thC, most examples of netting found today date from the 18thC and 19thC. Collectors often have to purchase a case first and the tools that go with it later. The piece illustrated measures 15cm (6in) in length, the top sliding over a slender cylinder in the base, rather than joining with an ivory screw thread, which would be susceptible to wear. The decorative carving depicts a snake catching a bird, with other birds in flight.

Eastern ivory netting case, c.1850, **£85–140/$135–225**

▼ Clamps

This ivory clamp is Cantonese in origin. While not a robust material, ivory was thought to have enough strength to make an effective pincushion clamp. The pressure the screw alone exerted in securing the clamp to a table was considerable, and it is quite rare to find one like this that has sustained no damage, although clearly it has been used. The carving is of birds, daisies and five male figures amid jungle foliage.

Cantonese ivory pin-cushion clamp, 1830–80, **£85–95/ $130–150**

Ivory

- Ivory is shiny, smooth and less dense than bone. (Bone is often distinguishable by its striations – the site of blood vessels when the bone was living.)
- Ivory often becomes brittle and yellows and warps with age so it should be cleaned and preserved with olive oil. It is porous and stains well.
- Ivorine and celluloid are both imitations of ivory.

▼ Etuis

The French ivory and gold etui illustrated below has suffered some wear. It has recesses specifically carved to take the particular tools it holds and, consequently, if damaged or lost these tools are almost impossible to replace. Particularly noteworthy is the fine clasp that closes the case. This etui contains a gold thimble decorated with pearls, steel and gold embroidery scissors and a stiletto, and a gold needle-case, needle and threader.

French ivory and gold etui, 1840–50, **£400–600/$640–960**

English treen needlebox, c.1840, **£185–250/$295–400**

▲ Boxes

This treen needlebox, with carved ivory tools, measures 15 x 10cm (6 x 4in) and is designed so that the tools unscrew from the top and are stored in the drawer. The drawer could also be used to store lace bobbins, tambour hooks, netting tools or a piece of embroidery work. The drawer handle and the feet are also of ivory. The tools are intended to represent a football pitch: the pin-cushion represents the ball; the needlecase, left, and thimble holder (containing an ivory thimble), right, are the goal posts; and the four reel holders form the net.

▶ Crochet & knitting accessories

In the 18thC and 19thC, knitting needle-ends and cases protected stitches when the work was stored. The ivory knitting needlecase shown is made in the form of sheep hooves. It held a set of four double-ended ivory knitting needles. The crochet hook, with engraved tail, features the owner's initials, "HC".

L to R: English ivory crochet hook, 1880–1920, **£5–10/$8–16**; knitting needlecase, c.1870, **£45–60/$70–95**

Tortoiseshell and silver etui, late 18thC–early 19thC, **£120–250/ $190–400**

▲ Cases

Tortoiseshell was used to make a variety of sewing accessories in the 18thC and 19thC. Thin slices were frequently used as a veneer on workboxes. It is a delicate material and prone to damage, hence accessories that have survived are fairly valuable today. The English etui shown measures 5.5 x 3cm (2¼ x 1¼in). It is decorated front and back with traditional silver swags and has a silver cartouche bearing initials on both sides. It holds miniature scissors, needles and a bodkin.

▼ "Piercy's Patent"

In the 19thC, Englishman John Piercy devised a method of combining tortoiseshell or horn with steel, iron, silver, gold or pinchbeck, which he patented in 1816. A number of sewing accessories were made by this process, but it is the rare thimble that is sought after. Thimbles carry the patent mark and generally have a dome of steel, silver or gold for strength.

English tortoiseshell, silver and gold thimble, c.1816, **£1,000–2,000/$1,600–3,200**

▼ Miniatures

It is quite difficult to replace tools that are missing from recessed compartments in a small box, but it is sometimes the box or sewing case itself that is worn out, with the tools still in good condition. That may have been the case with these seven mother-of-pearl miniatures, which were purchased as a set. Alternatively, each may have been used and not replaced in its designated container. It is sometimes worth purchasing tools to fit a box from an existing collection, but it is sensible to carry a pencil rubbing that shows the exact dimensions of the recess needing a tool, in order to make a perfect, or as near as perfect, match.

French miniature mother-of-pearl tools, c.1855, **£45–95/$70–150**

English mother-of-pearl sail boat thimble holder, 1900–1920, **£30–50/$50–80**

French spinet nécessaire, 1820–40, **£500–1,400/ $800–2,240**

▲ Thimble holders

Thimble holders as novelties were made in a large variety and are collectable in their own right and/or as a receptacle for a special thimble. This mother-of-pearl sail boat bears the words "A Present from Brighton" on one of the sails, and such pieces were at one time relatively expensive to buy at antiques fairs. Then several appeared on the scene and the price fell. Such is the risk with a collectable and it is why one should only collect for pleasure, rather than as a serious investment.

▶ Necessaires

This French rosewood musical spinet, right, with mother-of-pearl tools plays two Chopin pieces. There is a mirror on the inside of the lid and beneath the lid are four silk winders. The purple velvet lining provides a built-in pincushion. The other recessed compartments are lined with velvet and house a tambour hook, stiletto, needlecase, perfume bottle, thimble and scissors with gold decoration and a smocking tool, buttons and a penknife. The spinet is 15cm (6in) tall and 29 x 19cm (11½ x 7½in) at its widest. The curved side has three gilded brass decorations, the centre one including an escutcheon.

Scissors & sheaths

Prior to the 10thC scissors comprised two blades connected at one end to form a spring, as in sheep-shearing scissors today. From the 10thC onwards they were fashioned with bladed handles and a central pivot. By the mid-15thC their shape and decoration had begun to receive attention, and thinner, streamlined, engraved and damascened blades appeared. Beautiful yet functional scissors made a valuable and desirable gift for a wife or daughter. Some European examples imitated oriental models in their design; others were decorated with figures. Scissors with gold, enamel, silver or mother-of-pearl handles became prized possessions, particularly when encased in a decorative sheath for safety in transit.

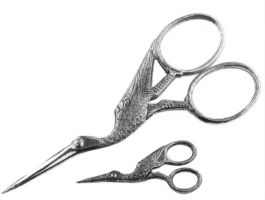

English stork scissors, c.1930, **£5–15/$8–24;** English miniature stork scissors, c.1900–10, **£30–45/ $50–70**

▲ Embroidery scissors
Originating in the East, stork scissors have been popular since the 19thC. Early producers were Sheffield-based, but Germany soon joined the market. Stork scissors were frequently found in workboxes. Illustrated above are stork embroidery scissors and the more unusual stork miniature scissors, the latter having their own leather case.

▼ Scissors in sheaths
These French scissors, made of silver gilt and steel, are typically delicate with graceful lines. They are encased in a tapering ormolu (gold-coloured metal alloy) sheath, measuring 10 x 3.5cm (4 x 1½in), with a ring on top with which to secure it to a chatelaine. The repoussé case is ornate, with a nymph riding a chariot on one side and a lady in similar fashion on the other. Bouquets and shooting stars appear overhead. It is easy to over-polish and dull an ormolu surface, so polish it only rarely with an impreg-nated dry cloth.

French embroidery scissors in an ormolu sheath, c.1820, **£120–160/ $190–255**

Above: English mother-of-pearl folding scissors, c.1880, **£25–45/ $40–70**; below: English folding scissors, c.1925, **£8–12/$13–19**

► **Folding scissors**
Folding or collapsible scissors were popular because they were easily transported and many fitted into etuis and hussifs. Intended for snipping thread, they are rarely robust and are sometimes quite awkward to fold down. The pair at the top are the earlier, with iron blades that fold into mother-of-pearl handles, making a width of 1.5cm (½in). The other pair are of a style still made today; their handles collapse to just 1cm (¼in) wide. More common now are handles that slide over the blades.

FACT FILE

Scissors
• In 14thC continental Europe a pair of scissors in a sheath, the latter of Muslim origin, would be given as a love token to a lady of noble birth.
• Early 20thC collapsible steel scissors had hinged handles, which folded down to be in line with their blades.

▼ **Damascened scissors**
From the late 19thC scissors were mass-produced, but they were also often decorated by hand. These two pairs of blue steel damascened scissors, below, were probably produced in Toledo, Spain, about 30 years apart. The design is chased in silver and gold. The pair on the right have gilded and decorated shanks and handles, with the blades decorated with birds and snakes in foliage. Similarly-decorated scissors were also produced in France, Italy and Germany.

Damascened scissors, 1870–1900, **£40–60/$65–95 (each)**

▼ **Enamel scissors**
These enamel scissors in a sheath, which have a matching thimble, were registered in 1924 under the mark of the Norwegian enameller David Andersen. Norway is a major cobalt ore-producing country, and cobalt is used extensively by Norwegian enamellers. These scissors have strong Pan-Slavic overtones – an interest Andersen developed while apprenticed to Jacob Tostrup, who trained in St Petersburg.

Norwegian enamel scissors in matching sheath, 1890–1900, **£150–200/$240–320**

Pincushions

In the 18thC ladies undertaking long coach journeys to visit friends and relatives took with them sewing accessories to effect repairs en route and provide amusement at their destination. The larger pincushions of the 16thC and 17thC were replaced with more convenient versions for carrying, often attached to chains of handmade cord to suspend them from the waistband. Small pinballs, covered in fine knitting and incorporating letters or numbers in sampler style, fetch high prices at auction today, if in good condition. By the reign of Queen Victoria needlework was in vogue, and this, coupled with the interest in extravagant design, resulted in a wide range of pincushions being produced.

L to R: silver shoe pincushion, Birmingham, 1917, **£80–120/ $130–190**; French ivory pincushion, 1820–60, **£45–80/$70–130**

▶ **Ivory & silver**
Elizabethan pincushions were often decorated with stumpwork. Later cushions became plainer, but the receptacles that held them were more decorative. The example above right, in a hand-painted ivory stand, is inscribed "A Friend's Gift". Roses and chain-stitch designs decorate the case and the base represents a daisy with red stamens. The silver shoe is hallmarked "Birmingham 1917". Pincushion holders were frequently made in the shape of swans, either in silver or a base metal, as here, with a huge price differential between the two.

Above: English metal swan pincushion, c.1928, **£15–25/ $24–40**

▼ **Bisque**
The 1920s bisque doll figure illustrated below has graceful limbs and is seated on the pincushion, which represents a bench. Pincushion dolls without legs are more common and were otherwise known as crinoline lady cushions, with the skirt serving as the cushion. When considering a purchase, the collector should ascertain that the skirt is original and not a cheap replacement.

German bisque pincushion, c.1920, **£60–90/$95–145**

Memorial pincushion, 1853–6,
£80–100/$130–160

▼ Advertising

Most frequently the labels on advertising novelties were for Dewhurst or Singer threads, and often the tool was shaped like a cotton reel. Generally, these items were not "give-aways" but were purchased specifically for use. The larger examples would have been used for advertising in draper's shops. Collectors of sewing accessories often extend their interest to collecting such advertising tools, sometimes even choosing to concentrate on them. Equally, collectors of advertising ware look for these pieces too. The result is increased competition and higher costs for the buyer. The older these advertising label novelties become, the more they are likely to be collected.

British advertising pincushion, 1930–50, **£5–15/$8–24**

▲ Commemorative

This memorial pincushion, 22 x 21cm (8¾ x 8¼in), is packed firmly with sawdust. It incorporates 2,128 pins into its design, each with a coloured, beaded post. It was made by a soldier or sailor, passing away his quieter hours during the Crimean War. Such cushions were often a gift for a wife, or the family of a deceased compatriot. They were not for use but display. Similar cushions were made by Native Americans, who adapted Victorian designs to fit their ceremonial traditions.

L to R: Tunbridge stickware pinwheel, 1840–60, **£65–95/$105–150**; English glass pinwheel, 1890s, **£35–65/$55–105**

▼ Pinwheels

Pincushions decreased in size from the 18thC until they reached the diminutive pinwheel in the Victorian era. Also known as pin discs, they consisted of two discs joined together, sometimes with a thin cushion sandwiched between them, as in the glass example shown below right. Alternatively the covered join took pins, as in the Tunbridge stickware version on the left. Each of these pinwheels measures 4.5cm (1¾in) in diameter. Be aware that items with pictures under glass are unstable, as age and wear can deteriorate the picture and cause it to break up.

Ancient and modern thimbles

Thimbles initially took the form of a piece of leather held over the thumb. Then came needle pushers, held in the palm of the hand, which were an improvement. Many museums claim ancient metal thimbles to be Roman, but the oldest known examples are 9th–12thC AD from Old Corinth. The metal thimble arrived in Europe from the East around the 9thC AD. In medieval times thimbles were either a ring, the precursor of the tailor's thimble today, used by exerting pressure with the side of the finger, or a beehive cap shape, which fitted the tip of the finger. The majority of working brass thimbles arrived in 17thC-Britain from Holland – Dutch maker John Lofting eventually brought the process to Britain in 1693.

Top: thimble ring, 11thC, **£35–100/ $55–160**; below: beehive thimble, 12thC, **£45–100/ $70–160**

▼ Ancient thimbles

The 900-year-old latten ring shown is one of the earliest thimbles known and is 0.6cm (¼in) deep. How its successor, the latten beehive, 1cm (½in) deep, was ever held on a finger tip is a mystery. Also designed to apply pressure from the side, it has a hole acquired during the casting process. The bronze Hispano-Moresque thimble, 4cm (1½in) high, would have been used when making saddles and harnesses. The bulbous Turkish thimble, 3cm (1in) deep, was used by exerting pressure on a needle from the side of the thumb.

L to R: Turkish thimble, 14thC, **£150–180/ $240–290**; Hispano-Moresque thimble, 12–13thC, **£95–120/ $150–190**

▶ Brass thimbles

Over the years, brass thimbles have generally been under-valued in collecting circles. Examples were produced using some of the designs found on their silver counterparts. Stronger and more affordable than silver, brass thimbles were found in the majority of workboxes until around the 1950s. This decorative example, top, is quite a rare design and has stems of bluebells around its border. Some 800 years after it first appeared, the thimble ring is now known as the tailor's thimble and is still produced, although normally by machine. However, this tailor's thimble is handmade, measuring 1cm (½in) in depth.

Above: English thimble, 1900–20, **£8–24/ $13–38**; below: tailor's thimble, 1940s, **£5–15/$8–24**

Left: Austrian Settmacher
petit-point thimble, c.1955,
£10–15/$16–24

Top right: Settmacher child's
thimble, c.1900; above:
ventilated thimble, early 20thC,
£10–25/$16–40 (each)

▲ **Base metal thimbles**

Most 20thC thimbles are
made of metal. Inexpensive
to mass-produce, many carry
designs also used on silver
thimbles. One of the world's
leading producers of metal
thimbles is Brüder Settmacher
of Vienna, founded in 1863.
Illustrated, top, is one of their
thimbles with petit-point decoration. Their silver-plated child's
thimble is 1cm (½in) deep and
1cm (½in) wide at the base.
The third thimble is an English
Charles Iles patent ventilated
thimble of cupro-nickel. The
first ventilated thimble was
patented as early as 1850.

▼ **Pewter thimbles**

Currently for sale as
modern souvenirs are
pewter thimbles, which
sell for just a few pounds
but are quite pleasing in
appearance. Pewter is an alloy,
usually of tin and lead, and
is fairly soft. It is not a viable
material, therefore, for a
thimble that is to be used
regularly, but the other essential
elements of a working thimble
(fit, shape, indentations and
lines) are present in some
pewter examples. This
particular thimble carries the
coat of arms of Poole, a resort
in southern England. Lesser
examples have the coat of
arms on a prominent shield,
which extends beyond the
lines of the thimble. They are,
and should be, cheap to buy.

English pewter thimble, modern,
£1.50–3/$2.50–5

FACT FILE

English "Just A Thimble Full", with
case, 1930–40, £12–35/$19–55

▲ **Thimble Fulls**

Not really thimbles at all,
but rather thimble-shaped,
these are measuring cups, or
beakers, for measuring spirits.
Thimble Fulls are collected
with sewing accessories
because of their thimble shape
and name. They were usually
sold with a designated case,
particularly the fragile glass
examples, but it is rare to find
one with a case today. This
1930s example, above, has
a case covered in red leather.
Thimble Fulls were produced
in glass, china, nickel silver,
silver plate, silver and also
gold, and in varying sizes.

Thimbles for display

In the 19thC attempts were made to produce glass thimbles which were both functional and decorative. Among the factories making them were those based on the island of Murano in Italy. Many such thimbles could in fact more accurately be described as "thimble shapes", but those that survive can claim a definite place in a thimble collection. When, in the latter part of the 18thC, the fashion for small wooden articles was at its height, thimbles in a variety of attractive woods were produced, often with matching cases. Since wood is soft and will not stand up to heavy use the fashion declined. However, those made from bog oak (a hard, dense wood) and of functional design were commonly used by Irish needlewomen of the time.

Right: Venetian thimble, late 20thC, **£18–25/$30–40**

▶ **Glass thimbles**
Some glass thimbles bear evidence of use. Providing the indentations on the dome are adequate, they may have been suited to working with fine fabrics. These two thimbles originate from Murano, Italy. The example dated 1885 is very rare but has undergone specialist reconstruction to repair it, which reduces its value. (In perfect condition it would be worth c.£1,000/ $1,600.) It is of made of layer upon layer of spun glass, the flowers added later. The blue glass and gold thimble, top, is recent and less rare.

Left: Venetian thimble (shape), 1885, **£100–150/ $160–240**

▼ **Glass Thimble Fulls**
From the late 19thC, the residue from completed items in a glass works was known as slag. This leftover material was available to workers who would fashion it, in their own time, into small items for their own use, called "whimsies". This is the origin of the slag-glass Thimble Full below, beautifully grained and vividly coloured in shades of turquoise and white. The words "Just A Thimble Full" are impressed on its border. Such pieces made from slag glass are quite rare.

English slag-glass Thimble Full, 1900–30, **£35–75/$55–120**

▼ Wooden thimbles

Wooden thimbles, like their glass equivalents, are impractical, being generally too soft to cope with the pressure of a needle. During the early years of Tunbridge ware, thimbles, along with clamps, boxes, reel cases, needlecases and thimble holders, were made as souvenirs. Old Tunbridge thimbles in good condition are fairly rare and consequently expensive to buy. However, there is always the hope that a naive stall-holder will not realise what the wooden thimble is sitting in the corner of their display case, or its true value.

English Tunbridge thimble, *c.*1820, **£150–200/$240–320**

Irish bog oak thimble, *c.*1930, **£50–85/$80–135**

▲ Bog oak thimbles

Not necessarily oak at all, bog oak is semi-petrified wood, found in Irish bogland and used to make souvenirs. Substantial numbers of black thimbles and other sewing accessories are normally made from bog oak, but the material has been known to be "faked", so beware. Wood stained black or, alternatively, bakelite was sometimes substituted for the real thing. Normally engraved, and often part of a matching set, the hard bog oak thimbles can stand up to some wear, providing they have indentations. This example is more of a thimble "shape" than other bog oak examples that collectors may come across.

From the mid-19thC celluloid, bakelite and, later, plastic thimbles appeared, chiefly in the USA. Many a novice collector has bought an early cream example as an ivory thimble, at ivory prices. A 1930s and 1940s fashion in the USA was to decorate them with hand-painted or transfer designs, but the images rubbed off with wear. In good condition such thimbles are fairly costly to buy.

▼ Decorated plastic thimbles

Thimbles bearing advertising slogans, such as the example below left, are not readily available in the UK, although occasionally early 20thC bakelite versions do emerge. The other thimble is a copy of a well-known American silver thimble, with images of cupids around its intact border; it is worth a great deal more than the average plastic thimble.

Left: American plastic thimble, 1984, **£3–5/$5–8**

Right: American plastic thimble, *c.*1910, **£30–45/ $50–70**

Porcelain & precious thimbles

Intended as love tokens for display rather than use, fine hand-decorated porcelain thimbles can form a collection in their own right. Meissen was the first factory, in the 18thC, to produce porcelain thimbles. Their shape and decoration are distinctive and relatively few were made – one was sold in 1997 for £8,000 ($12,800). From the late 18thC to mid-20thC, the Royal Copenhagen, Chelsea, Royal Worcester and Derby factories were among those producing quality thimbles, and these are prized by collectors today. Thimbles were also made as love tokens in the 19thC, and were of mother-of-pearl, enamel, gold or jewel-encrusted. When such a thimble appears for sale it frequently has some damage, as many have been used. Those that are still in good condition reach high prices in the salerooms.

Royal Worcester, c.1865, £150–250/$240–400; Meissen, 1999, £65–95/$105–150

◀ Porcelain
Of the many porcelain factories producing thimbles in the late 18thC and 19thC, Royal Worcester was one of the best, and its hand-painted images are surpassed by none. In the late 20thC the factory used transfer designs instead of hand-painted ones, before finally stopping its production of thimbles altogether. Shown here, top, is an 1860s Royal Worcester hand-painted thimble on a blush-coloured background. This example has no back stamp (maker's mark) to identify it as Royal Worcester. The other thimble is a design by Meissen for a 1999 thimble – possibly the only one specially produced for the last year of the previous millennium.

▼ Bone china
In the 20thC, Royal Worcester thimbles were made in bone china (soft paste), rather than porcelain. The standard of their artists (in many cases several members of the same family) continued to be excellent. Shown top right is a signed thimble with a beautifully hand-painted kingfisher sitting on reeds by a river. Other images popularly used at this time included fruit and flowers. The thimble has a black back stamp inside. Pictured below is an inexpensive bone-china transfer thimble issued by "elgate" Products Ltd to celebrate the year 2000. Illustrated in the background is the Millennium Dome at Greenwich, London.

Royal Worcester, c.1950, £10–35/$16–55; "elgate", 1999, £1–2/$1.50–3

"Palais Royal" pansy thimble,
1840–60, **£250–400/$400–640**

▲ **Mother-of-pearl**
Few thimbles were made in
mother-of-pearl because the
material lacked the required
strength to push a needle
though fabric. It is remarkable
that craftsmen were able to
fashion indentations of any
kind on those that were made.
Gold banding usually forms
a border around these
thimbles, which gives some
support. The thimble shown
is the very best example,
bearing the coveted yellow
enamel pansy, synonymous
with the quality of Palais
Royal craftmanship. An
identical thimble of the
same provenance but without
the pansy would be less
expensive. Generally, these
thimbles were intended to be
included in French necessaires
and workboxes.

▼ **Enamel**
Skilled Norwegian enamellers
frequently completed some of
their training in Germany and
Austria, hence their shared
technique of finely guilloched
(machine-tooled) backgrounds.
The silver thimble with hand-
painted enamel border and
purple glass stone top is
typically German, and was
made by Friedrich Eber in
Pforzheim. The silver and
maker's marks, together with
the size, are visible above the
border in this photograph.
The other thimble is an
example of Norwegian
silhouette enamelling (see
p.22) and was made by the
David Andersen company.
Original examples with
moonstone tops, such as
this, are very collectable.

German silver
and enamel
thimble,
c.1925,
**£50–80/
$80–130**

Norwegian
silhouette
enamel
thimble,
1890–1900,
**£65–375/
$105–600**

Palais Royal
Occasionally a mother-
of-pearl thimble is found
that cannot easily be
defined as Palais Royal.
Sometimes shaped like
an average thimble in use
today, they are generally
modern, inexpensive and
frequently come from
Eastern and Mediterranean
countries, where they are
sold as souvenirs. Though
rare, antique alternatives
to Palais Royal do exist.

French gold
and enamel
thimble,
1820–40,
**£200–350/
$320–560**

Israeli thimble
with garnets,
1980,
**£35–70/
$55–110**

▲ **Jewelled**
Gold thimbles decorated with
real or imitation jewels served
as expensive gifts in the 18thC
and 19thC. The beehive-
shaped thimble shown contains
four enamel "turquoise" stones;
real turquoise discolours and
therefore was rarely used.
Silver thimbles were also
adorned, either around a
skirted border or on top. More
attractive than practical is this
Israeli example with "garnets"
(crimson-tinted almandines).

Silver & gold thimbles

An increase in trade between continents in the 16thC made precious metals more widely available. By the mid-18thC, silver thimbles fashioned by specialist makers were plentiful. Prominent English makers in the 19thC were Charles Horner, Henry Griffiths, James Fenton, Samuel Foskett and James Swann. Under a 1738 Act of Parliament silver thimbles were exempt from hall-marking, until the practice was reintroduced in 1885. Gold and silver-gilt thimbles were probably first seen in early 18thC France, then Britain and, later, the USA. Individually made by jewellers, the average cost then was around 50 shillings, but there were more expensive British and European examples of different shades of gold, adorned with precious and semi-precious stones. Many survived in mint condition, suggesting that they were treasured and displayed, not used.

L to R: "Atlantic cable" thimble, c.1860, **£35–50/ $55–80**; US cupid thimble, 1906, **£80–120/ $130–190**

▶ **Silver**
The English "Atlantic cable" thimble shown here has a fluted fleur-de-lys skirt and tooled border. In 1866 an identical thimble, now in London's Science Museum, helped send the first transatlantic cable signal from Ireland to Newfoundland. The American silver cupid thimble by Simon Brothers was patented in 1906; other US companies such as Ketcham McDougall and Henry Webster also produced this cupid design.

▼ **Ornate silver**
This late 18thC English silver filigree (wirework) thimble, below left, was made in Birmingham. Frequently part of a compendium including a scent bottle and tape measure or needlecase and seal, such pieces were originally regarded as toys. Indian thimbles, such as the one on the right, are quite distinctive: tall and slender, they are ornately engraved and embossed with flowers, some with a scalloped edge. They were imported to Britain or brought back as souvenirs. They are not yet too difficult to find in Britain and the USA.

L to R: English filigree thimble, late 18thC, **£135–175/$215–280**; Indian thimble, c.1880, **£75–130/$120–210**

L to R: American scenic thimble, c.1900, **£80–120/$130–190**; English gold "wedding" thimble, c.1820, **£210–300/$340–480**

FACT FILE

The Dorcas thimble

The maximum working life of only 20 years for a silver thimble concerned makers so they experimented with iron and steel caps. In 1884 Halifax jeweller Charles Horner patented the successful Dorcas thimble, steel-cored and dipped in silver – guaranteed for a lifetime.

▼ "Dorcas"

Many thimbles from the late 19thC that are believed to be silver are in fact steel-cored. In 1884, Charles Horner patented the "Dorcas", which came in its own labelled cardboard box. Other named designs followed, such as the "Louise", "Diamond", "Princess May" and "Shell". Horner was granted an American patent in 1889 to produce thimbles for the USA. Inexperienced dealers often offer Dorcas (and similar) thimbles as silver. Test them: a steel-cored thimble will attract a magnet, a silver one will not.

Two steel-cored Dorcas thimbles, c.1887, one in perfect condition (right), the other worn, showing steel core, **£5–18/$8–30**

▲ Gold

Of all the American gold thimbles produced, the scenic examples are possibly the most interesting. The 10-carat (karat) thimble illustrated above left was made by Simons Brothers, its border of buildings engraved and chased by hand. On the reverse side, a cartouche bears the initials "IMB". Above right is a three-coloured gold thimble, with an embossed band suggesting a wedding ring, hence its name.

▼ Gold-coated

The thimble below left was designed in 1986 in England by James Swann and was one of several prototypes submitted to record the 400th anniversary of Amsterdam as a diamond city. It is of silver gilt. Alas, it was not chosen. Beneath it is an American gold-filled thimble by Simons Brothers, with a trefoil mark and a scrolled edge. Gold-filled thimbles are difficult to distinguish from gold, except by testing, as there is no hall-marking system in the USA.

Above: silver gilt thimble, 1990, **£110–130/$175–210**; right: American gold-filled thimble, c.1930, **£45–65/$70–105**

Thimble holders

Treasured thimbles in the 18thC and 19thC were kept in designated containers – either the cardboard box or leather case in which they were supplied or, more usually, in a case specifically made to house a thimble and sometimes purchased separately. The container was usually worth less than the thimble, but as much care was normally taken over the making of holders as over most sewing accessories. Designs usually reflected the period of manufacture: a copy of a contemporary velvet ladies' shoe, for example. Thimble holders in Mauchline ware were often inscribed with the words "A Present From ...", and sold as souvenirs. Some holders took the form of a novelty – a brass or mother-of-pearl egg, a miniature monument or chest, or a sailing boat (see p.29) – the variety was endless.

▼ American

This American thimble holder, fashioned as a Japanese geisha, is very delicate and made from almost paper-thin celluloid. On her back, the bustle matches perfectly when the top and bottom of the case are correctly aligned. The sweetgrass basket holder was made on a Native American reservation. Native Americans also made other tools from woven sweet-grass – scissor sheaths and pincushions among them.

Above: celluloid holder, c.1925, **£20–50/ $32–80**; below: Native American straw holder, c.1910, **£15–25/$24–40**

▼ English

The thimble holder lent itself well to tourist souvenir ware. The alabaster from which the monument holder, right, is made simulates marble and holds an Austrian silver-plate thimble with copper lining from the period. It is inscribed "A Present from Bournemouth". The shoe holder is made of typically Victorian purple velvet, its sole and heel stiffened with lead. Embroidered flowers on the front of the shoe simulate beadwork. The holder carries a small brass thimble of the same period, which has an attractive floral border.

Above: marble holder, c.1930, **£20–35/$30– 55**; below: velvet shoe, c.1890, **£30– 50/$50–80**

Bavarian bear holder/pincushion, c.1920, **£15–35/$24–55**

▲ German

This fairly crude tin bear holds a small brass thimble. Attached to him is a pin-cushion, its metal base originally painted green. Made in Bavaria in the early 20thC, these bears, which came in various sizes, have recently attracted much interest from collectors, causing the prices to rise. When buying such a holder, the collector must be certain that the bear's paws will secure a thimble, as many have become distorted over the years.

▼ Vegetable ivory

Vegetable ivory is one of the strongest materials from which sewing tools were made. Its sheen, subtle change of colour through ageing and the beautiful turning involved in making accessories endear it to collectors. The top example, a simple but graceful design, is made from corozo nut, the true vegetable ivory. The classic acorn shape of the other has been turned from the coquilla nut, which ranges from sienna to a darker brown. It is frequently referred to as vegetable ivory, which is a popular misconception.

Vegetable ivory holder, 1860–90, **£35–65/$55–105**

Coquilla nut holder, 1860–90, **£35–65/$55–105**

Mother-of-pearl holder, c.1920, **£20–50/$32–80**

▲ French

This mother-of-pearl holder, lined with now-faded felt, is often incorrectly referred to by stall-holders as a purse. It is strengthened by its gilded edging which clasps together the two shells. "A Present from Ostende" has been inscribed by hand. It was a very popular design, with various assumed uses. Many are now appearing at antiques fairs and selling for less than the estimated price of this case. Similar but more recent designs from horn, turtle and various other shells are also surfacing. None of these modern cases is lined.

Finger & nail guards

Finger guards, also known as shields or protectors, were frequently used in the Victorian era. English examples resemble a thimble with the back cut away; Continental guards had a large shield-shaped front and a ring back. Sewing boxes from the 18thC and 19thC normally contained both a thimble and a finger guard, usually of matching design and made of silver, silver gilt or even ivory, enamel and/or gold. More costly examples often came in their own box, with a thimble and sometimes a tape measure. Guards were worn on the index finger of the hand not holding a needle. In the mid-20thC, simple celluloid and plastic finger guards were often used by those finishing fine garments by hand.

▶ **Silver**

The English guard shown right typically has a matching thimble (not pictured) and is from the mid-19thC. The bevelled top protects the nail. European finger guards are entirely different from their English counterparts, but fulfil the same function. This example, below right, extends beyond the tip of a nail, offering protection from the point of a needle whilst sewing. Designs similar to European guards were produced in the USA.

Above: English silver guard, c.1860, **£60–80/$95–130**; below: Dutch silver guard, c.1830, **£80–120/$130–190**

▼ **Plastic**

The practice of using finger guards or shields when sewing continued well into the 20thC. Shown left are two plastic guards. The top example is slightly cumbersome in design, with ridged edges that must have interfered with the fabric being sewn. This sort of guard was sometimes used as a ventilated thimble. The other example, made of imitation tortoiseshell and with rounded edges, was much more viable for practical use.

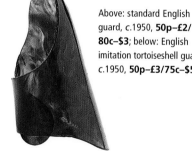

Above: standard English guard, c.1950, **50p–£2/80c–$3**; below: English imitation tortoiseshell guard, c.1950, **50p–£3/75c–$5**

Nail guards

Also known as "protectors" are the three Eastern temple dancers' nail guards shown below. Two are enamel on silver, the third (in the centre) is on silver plate. The example on the right is in filigree work with imitation "jewels". The guards were usually made of silver or gold and supplied in sets of ten, but today they are normally found singly. They are not sewing accessories, but are collected simply because they were worn on the finger. The two longer examples both measure 9cm (3½in) in height.

Three temple dancers' enamelled nail guards, 1890, **£40–80/ $65–130**

Wigmaker's finger guard, 20thC, **£3–5/$5–8**

▲ Craftsmen's finger guards

Craftsmen also needed guards to protect their fingers and nails, and generally these served an additional function, as does the example shown here. This shiny steel guard is used by wigmakers. The pointed tip lifts the base canvas onto which the hair is sewn, thus enabling the craftsman to attach the hair securely with his needle.

Other finger guards

Finger guards are also worn for safety in various jobs, ranging from rubber finger stalls, which are thimble-shaped and grip paper (bank notes, for example) when it is being counted, to metal finger protectors, which are used in certain manual occupations (*see* below).

FACT FILE

▼ Thatchers' finger guards

This example is of a thatcher's finger guard, made of tin, which was (and is) worn in sets of ten. As progress is made in thatching a roof the thatcher's helper has the job of sorting the straw to be used. Nails are very prone to damage by straw ends and the rubbish that gets caught up in it. Craftsmen's and thatchers' guards, and others, only qualify for inclusion in a sewing accessories collection because they are used to protect fingers.

Thatcher's finger guard, 20thC, **£3–5/$5–8**

Tape measures

King Henry VII of England introduced a King's Standard of measurement in the 15thC, but it was not until the 20thC that a universally recognized form of measurement was achieved. An English "yard" (0.91m/3ft) was introduced in the 16thC. The final 2¼ inches (5.5cm) of the yard was known as a "nail" and by 1905 brass measures, calibrated in nails, were still being used by some shopkeepers. Until the 19thC Europe used the "ell" (1.15m/ 3ft 9in) as a rough measurement for fabric, ostensibly based on the rather changeable distance from elbow to fingertips or shoulder to wrist! When the length of a cloth tape needed verification in the early 19thC, it was held against a Yard Rule at the town's guildhall. The British introduced the Imperial Standard Yard in 1885 and the USA adopted it one year later.

German brass wind-up tape, c.1920, **£60–100/ $95–160**

▼ Brass
The beautifully embossed brass wind-up measure illustrated top is known in the USA as a Napkin Ring. The initials on top, "DRGM", identify it as German and made after 1918. It carries the registration number 55976. Tape measurement is hand-painted in inches on one side and centimetres on the other. The tape below, also brass, has a spring action. The illustration, under celluloid, shows Alexandra Palace in north London.

▼ Plastic and coquilla nut
The English plastic spring-action tape measure can be dated by the picture of the wire-haired fox terrier, which was popular in the first 30 to 40 years of the 20thC. The other example is a wind-up tape, possibly Indian, with detailed carving. The winding spindle, as well as the handle of the tape, is of ivory. The roof and main body are in two shades of brown coquilla nut. The tape is calibrated in "nails".

Above: plastic, spring-action tape, c.1930, **£12–25/$19– 40**; below: ivory/coquilla nut wind-up tape, early 19thC, **£25– 45/$40–70**

English brass spring-action tape measure, c.1930, **£15–25/ $24–40**

French silver wind-up
tape, c.1825,
£50–95/$80–150

- Tapes were generally imported from France until the mid-19thC and found in fitted needlework boxes. They were usually marked in handwritten inches for the UK market.
- Cottage industries made or assembled tapes in Britain from the mid-19thC. Some measures were still imported from other countries.

▲ Silver

This tiny and beautifully embossed silver wind-up tape measure from the early 19thC measures 2.5 x 1.5cm (1 x ½in) and would have been part of a set, with a matching thimble and emery/pincushion. The tape is calibrated in inches only. The case was probably made in France and assembled in an English cottage industry (employees working from home, often using their own equipment). The design of this tape measure has Indian overtones – a style that was very popular in the 19thC. Other silver examples from this period are plainer and sometimes take the form of an animal, such as a dog, cat or perhaps a pig. These silver pieces are, inevitably, expensive to buy. Reproductions in composite metal do appear on the market and collectors should note that if a piece claims to be genuine silver, it normally carries a clear hallmark.

English treen wind-up tape, c.1900,
£25–40/$40–65

▲▶ Wooden

The spring-action tape measure below right features Muffin the Mule, from the English 1950s children's television programme of that name. Here, Muffin is supported by a barrel, which contains the tape. His head is fixed by a spring, allowing it to nod as the tape is used. The example above is of a treen wind-up tape measure, calibrated only in inches and marked by hand. The lever that winds the tape is of brass. The tape measure is 3cm (1¼in) in diameter.

English wooden novelty "Muffin the Mule" spring-action tape, c.1950, **£25–35/$40–55**

Items of geographical origin

The types of sewing tools pictured on these pages are known by the name of the region in which they originated. Tunbridge ware derived its name from a town in Kent for which it was manufactured. Mauchline ware is the generic name for Scottish souvenir ware, produced from the mid-19thC until 1933, when the principal factory was destroyed by fire. It came in several distinctive styles: tartan ware, photographic transfer ware, photographic ware and fernware; black lacquer, seaweed, coloured fern-ware and Christmas ware were also produced in smaller quantities. Wooden sewing accessories such as these were not only intended for decoration, but were extensively used; proof of their quality is that many have survived for over 100 years. Scarcity and mint condition cause some tools to command high prices.

Stickware needlecase, c.1860, **£60–85/$95–135**

◀ **English Tunbridge ware**
Illustrated left are two examples of Tunbridge ware, made during the 19thC. The needlecase's front cover is in mosaic stickware technique and the back cover in a cube pattern known as tumbling blocks – both designs introduced after 1840. The inside of the case is edged with stickware banding. Below is a combination piece of the rarer pre-1840 Tunbridge ware. It comprises a pincushion, thimble holder and wax holder.

▼ **Scottish tartan ware**
The older needlecase on the left has seen much wear. Its covering is of a simpler tartan design than that on the bodkin case. At the time these pieces were made, the design was "woven" on to the paper and the basic wooden tool covered with the paper. Many tartans were used, both genuine and invented. In later versions the quality of workmanship was poorer, with black lines disguising bad joins.

L to R: tartan ware needle-case, c.1860, **£45–75/ $70–120**; bodkin case, c.1880, **£50– 95/$80–150**

Early Tunbridge pincushion combination, c.1800, **£125–185/$200–295**

▼ Scottish photographic & transfer ware

Mauchline souvenir ware was made from 1850 to 1933. As holiday souvenirs, each piece of photographic and transfer ware carried an image of the location. In the late 19thC the product was exported to France and elsewhere. Below is a combination emery and pincushion, the transfer entitled "St Mary Church, Reading". The thimble holder is decorated in photographic ware; the image is of "The "Gardens, Bournemouth".

Above: emery/pincushion combination, c.1880, **£55–85/ $90–135**; below: thimble holder, c.1890, **£55–85/$90–135**

Above: Christmas pincushion, c.1920, **£65–90/$105–145**; below: fern-ware pincushion, c.1890, **£60–85/$95–135**

▲ Christmas ware & Scottish fern ware

A rare version of transfer ware, and in colour, this heart-shaped pincushion was a gift from a gentleman to his lady. On the front is a holly wreath, wishing the recipient "A Merry Christmas". On the reverse, a robin sits amid holly branches with "A Happy Christmas" written beneath. Below is a pinwheel in fern-ware, manufactured from 1870. This decoration was made using a fern frond as a stencil. The whole cushion was then varnished.

Tunbridge ware

Tunbridge ware, produced from the 17thC, was at first distinguished by its fine turning. From the 19thC a pale wood was used, decorated with fine lines of green, red, yellow and/or black. Mosaic stickware technique (banded inlays cut from laminated blocks) was popular from 1840.

▼ Irish bog oak

This cauldron-shaped thimble holder is carved with Irish clover leaves and is unlined. It was one of a number of bog oak accessories that were popular in the 1920–30s, including pincushions in the shape of saucepans, chairs, Bishop's thrones, top hats and cauldrons on a fire. More properly it might have been named bog wood, since it is derived from various types of tree, blackened through immersion in Irish bog water.

Irish bog oak thimble holder, c.1920, **£50–65/$80–105**

Finishing tools

Needlewomen were the source of many new ideas for sewing accessories, and would have instructed craftsmen as to which tools they would find useful in their craft. One of the most popular inventions must have been the clamp, which originated in the early 19thC. The hemming bird, which could be attached to a table, is possibly the best known clamp, patented in the USA in 1853. Prior to mass-production, cloth was expensive and repairs gave added life to linen and garments – particularly socks and stockings. Egg-shaped darners are generally pre-20thC; those that are mushroom-shaped are later. Some unscrew to reveal a needlecase in the stem; others are novelties. Usually 15cm (6in) in length, hem measures have been popular since the 19thC, enabling hems to be sewn evenly. Silver varieties of these measures are normally American.

▼ Clamps

The hemming-bird clamp shown here is an original patented example. The leafy design on the brass ware is clear and crisp and the pincushions are original, in now-faded purple velvet. The clamp was fixed to a table and material snapped in its spring-loaded beak, leaving the hands free to stitch the hem. Older examples are fairly heavy and modern pieces lighter. The rose-wood clamp is simply a pincushion. There were clamps for other jobs, including winding and netting.

American brass hemming bird, c.1860, **£95–125/ $150–200**

English rosewood pincushion, c.1840, **£60–80/$95–130**

▼ Darners

This American darner has a repoussé silver handle and a black "egg". Whilst material might slip off the egg during darning, it at least did not damage fine fabric during repair. At 16cm (6¼in), it is longer than a European darner, which averaged 12cm (4¾in). Painted on the wooden mushroom-shaped darner below is a heart. It is probably Dutch in origin. Many darners were plastic, though wooden examples were more effective. Other versions, for specific purposes, appeared in the 1940s and 1950s.

Above: American darner, c.1900, **£40–80/$65–130**; below: Continental darner, c.1950, **£1.50–8/$2.50–13**

▼ Hem measures

These multi-functional scissors, left, were made in Germany by Efka in the early 1920s. At the top is a velvet marker and, on one handle, a hole to string a pencil. The mother-of-pearl shanks have serrations to grip and open a screw top. The blades are calibrated in inches and centimetres. The dual-function American hem measure, right, is calibrated in 4 inches (10cm). The embossed pattern on the head is repeated on the sliding cutter, which made buttonholes.

German multi-functional scissors, 1920s, **£50–95/ $80–150**

▼ Button holers

The American ornate brass button holer shown here has an extremely sharp pointed blade, which is calibrated in centimetres. The steel blade can be pushed down to the calibration, which corresponds with the desired width of the buttonhole, enabling all the holes to be the same size. It is stamped "DMC & Co. Pat Sept [19]37 BPT Conn". Other sewing accessories in brass can be found that are similar in style to this button holer; a collector may wish to find closely matching tools to equip a sewing box or table of the same period. The scissors shown below right have a screw adjustment, which can pre-determine the size of buttonholes. Although they perform their function, these scissors are not as efficient as their brass counterpart.

Left: American silver hem measure, c.1925, **£40–75/ $65–120**

Buttonholes

Creating neat button-holes was achieved in the 19thC using one of two accessories:
• The buttonhole cutter. Usually brass, these had calibrations alongside a retractable sharp blade.
• Buttonhole scissors. These are still manu-factured, but in chrome as opposed to the older steel versions. These frequently had a screw adjustment to determine and set the measurement of the buttonholes.

L to R: American button holer, 1937, **£45–85/$70–135**; English buttonhole scissors, modern, **£3–12/$5–19**

Tools for adorning

There was no more popular a time for adornment than during the Victorian era (1837–1901). Household ware, garments and needlework all received a decorative treatment, with frills and edgings in vogue, each one more frivolous than the next. The range of tools used was large, but of particular significance were stilettos and tatting shuttles. Stilettos had a rounded steel blade tapering to a point, used for making design holes in fabric. Tatting shuttles were invariably hand-carved, inlaid or carried an inscription. Rings and frames held fabric taut for working tiny stitches, the most portable being two rings, one inside the other. Table- and floor-standing frames of polished mahogany, rosewood or yew were superior in finish and more sturdy than is generally the case today.

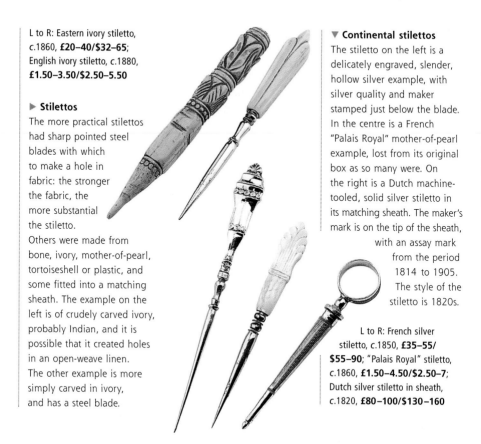

L to R: Eastern ivory stiletto, c.1860, **£20–40/$32–65**; English ivory stiletto, c.1880, **£1.50–3.50/$2.50–5.50**

▶ **Stilettos**
The more practical stilettos had sharp pointed steel blades with which to make a hole in fabric: the stronger the fabric, the more substantial the stiletto. Others were made from bone, ivory, mother-of-pearl, tortoiseshell or plastic, and some fitted into a matching sheath. The example on the left is of crudely carved ivory, probably Indian, and it is possible that it created holes in an open-weave linen. The other example is more simply carved in ivory, and has a steel blade.

▼ **Continental stilettos**
The stiletto on the left is a delicately engraved, slender, hollow silver example, with silver quality and maker stamped just below the blade. In the centre is a French "Palais Royal" mother-of-pearl example, lost from its original box as so many were. On the right is a Dutch machine-tooled, solid silver stiletto in its matching sheath. The maker's mark is on the tip of the sheath, with an assay mark from the period 1814 to 1905. The style of the stiletto is 1820s.

L to R: French silver stiletto, c.1850, **£35–55/$55–90**; "Palais Royal" stiletto, c.1860, **£1.50–4.50/$2.50–7**; Dutch silver stiletto in sheath, c.1820, **£80–100/$130–160**

L to R: English mock tortoiseshell rings, c.1910, **£15–35/$24–55**; English wooden clamp, c.1935, **£10–25/$16–40**

▲ Embroidery rings

Embroidery rings are used as much today as ever they were, and their design has not changed significantly. These examples are early 20thC. The model on the left is plasticized tortoiseshell and has two rings, one fitting into the other. "The Perfect Grip, British Patent 30746" is stamped on the outer ring. The inner ring has grooves on the outside to grip the fabric securely. The clamped version, right, still popular today, leaves both hands free to work with the needle or hook. To improve the efficiency of this latter example, cotton fabric such as a bandage was wound around and secured to the inner ring. This helped to grip the fabric being worked without distorting its texture or rubbing a transfer-printed design.

Tatting

Tatting, which resembles fine crochet, reached its height in popularity in the mid-19thC. A tatting shuttle consists of two oval shapes, tapering at each end and joined at their centres. The tips did not always touch until the late 19thC, and collectors who shun those with open ends miss out on rare early examples.

▼ Tatting shuttles

Tatting shuttles came in mother-of-pearl, ivory, tortoiseshell, bone, plastic, wood, Mauchline ware (transfer, photographic, fern and tartan ware – see below right) and silver and gold (sometimes enamelled). The ivory example on the left carries the beginnings of a piece of tatting. Both shuttles measure 7cm (2¾in) in length. Early shuttles were often intricately carved and impractical for their purpose. Cases designed to hold shuttles also had sections for scissors, a purling pin (to join the loops), cotton, perhaps a spool knave and a needle-case. Larger shuttles were used for knotting rather than tatting.

L to R: ivory shuttle, c.1890, **£15–40/ $24–65**; tartan-ware shuttle, c.1870, **£55–95/$90–150**

Associated accessories

In addition to the more commonly found sewing accessories, there are a number of items that are more specialist, of which fewer were made but that nevertheless form a legitimate part of any sewing collection: lyre-shaped lucets of smooth wood, bone or ivory, used to make cord for garments and soft bags, or for suspending tools from a waistband; crochet hooks, made of silver, steel, base metal, bone or ivory – sometimes engraved, often collapsible and illustrated with advertisements; tambour hooks of gold or silver, often jewelled; antique bobbins of wood, bone or ivory, used in pairs to make lace, and commanding high prices when decorated or inscribed; needles and meshes, the tools of netting (which was handmade until mechanization cut costs in the mid-19thC), stored in carved bone or ivory cases, or in boxes.

▼ Lucets

The lucet was a tool used to make cord. Those competent in both tatting and lucet work used rapid hand movements, the tool flashing as it worked. The ivory example, left, shows the way it was threaded to produce the cord. Both lucets illustrated are English and each measures 10 x 4cm (4 x 1½in).

L to R: English ivory lucet, c.1860, **£45–90/ $70–145;** English treen lucet, c.1920, **£30–50/ $50–80**

▶ Tambour hooks

It is essential when buying a tambour hook to ensure it still has at least one hook fitted and, preferably, is in its case. Ideally it should have three to four hooks of differing sizes. This example hails from Dieppe, whose craftsmen were well known for their ivory carving. The wing nut, which releases the hook, is shown, as is the top, which protects the delicate end. Tambour hooks are normally expensive, as they are fairly rare and were usually made of costly materials – mother-of-pearl, silver and gold – and were sometimes enamelled and/or "jewelled".

Dieppe ivory tambour hook, c.1840, **£65–100/$105–160**

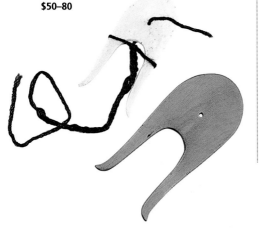

Tambouring

Popular in the Georgian period (1714–1830), tambouring was revived in the Victorian era. Semi-transparent fabric, held taut by a frame, was pierced by a tiny tambour hook, creating a chain stitch from the reverse side – used to decorate garments and white work as well as to embroider.

FACT FILE

▼ Crochet hooks

Of these six crochet hooks, two are English (second and third left) and four American – the latter rarely seen in Europe. Third from left is a long and large tricot hook in ivory and treen, measuring 27cm (10½in). It held the worked stitches and is also known as an Afghan or Tunisian hook. The rest of the hooks average 11cm (4¼in). The first and second right are collapsible, the hook retracting into the main body for protection. If a base metal hook is rusty, restore it by soaking it for twenty-four hours in a penetrating engine oil.

Crochet hooks, 1870–1900, **£3.50–12/$5.50–19 each**

English bobbins (L to R): wooden, 1900, **£15–20/$24–32**; ivory, c.1840, **£30–90/$50–145**; stained ivory, c.1850, **£25–60/$40–95**

▲ Lace bobbins

Laid on a piece of antique lace above are three English bobbins, all of which are very collectable. The wooden example has been wired for strength. The ivory bobbin in the centre has been hand-painted. The name "William" is etched in poker work and was probably the lace maker's child or sweetheart. On the right is another ivory bobbin, this time stained in red, a fashion of the time. Bobbins that were commemorative or carried names are always more expensive than plain ones.

Right: (L to R) English part set, c.1880–1910, **10p–£3/15c–$5 each**; faceted steel clamp, c.1840, **£35–70/$55–110**

▼ Netting tools

Below is a selection of needles and meshes that were used to make netting for personal use. They are often found singly or in couples, but rarely as a complete set. However, individually they are generally inexpensive and many stall-holders do not know what they are. To their right is a 19thC faceted steel clamp with a hook on top, which secured one end of the net while it was fashioned.

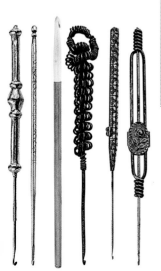

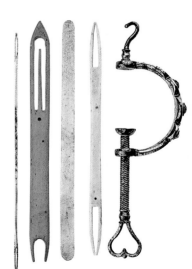

Extending a collection

Collections frequently include examples of fine needlework and items other than sewing accessories that were to be found in 18thC and 19thC workboxes. Samplers on fine fabric, often worked by children practising stitchery, command four-figure sums if they have the desired attributes: bright colours, a stitched house, a tree, a bird, the alphabet, numbers, the name of the maker and a date. Other items in workboxes were generally things that might be useful during a visit away from home: scent bottles, game counters, stamps, penknives and knitting tools. Wool was frequently wound onto small flat hand-winders from hanks, using a table or floor-standing wool winder. These winders are still used today and are found in many collections.

Right: English sampler, 1885, **£100–185/ $160–295**

▶ **Samplers**
Samplers demonstrated one's ability in embroidery stitchery. They often gave an insight into the maker's life, but without the name, and the date it was completed, worked into them they are worth much less. So often samplers have been exposed to the light and their colours have faded. If they are displayed, it should be well away from a window to avoid light damage. The sampler pictured reads that it was completed by "Ethel Deakin, aged 12. 1885".

▼ **Game counters & penknives**
The engraved mother-of-pearl game counter shown heralds from Canton in China. There would have been a number in the set – oblong, round or oval in shape. This one shows a man washing his feet in the central circle, flanked by bouquets. On the reverse, a swan appears in the circle. The beautiful brass penknife is daintily engraved. Both would have had their place in workboxes of the 18thC and 19thC.

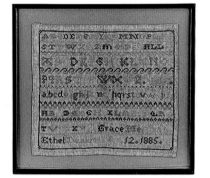

Above: Cantonese mother-of-pearl game counter, c.1860, **£5–10/ $8–16**; below: English brass pen-knife, 1890s, **£15–35/$24–55**

L to R: Spanish wooden knitting needle sheath, c.1880, **£95–135/$150–215**; Irish marquetry sheath, 1885, **£120–165/$190–265**

▲ Knitting needle sheaths

Knitting was an important cottage industry, but with mechanization in the18thC it withdrew to the more remote areas of Britain, such as Shetland off the coast of Scotland, where the fastest knitters were found and where knitting is still an occupation. A sheath securing the right-hand needle allowed the knitter to concentrate on the work of the left hand, thus speeding up the process. The sheaths above are both of wood and of similar vintage. On the left is a Spanish version and on the right is a fine example of Irish marquetry. Newarke House Museum, Leicester, has a sheath from as early as 1628.

▶ Wool winders

Two different winders are shown here. Above is a German table-top example in steel, with heads – half lion, half man – moulded on the base. The cup at the top, which holds a ball of wool, is of blue-and-white porcelain. Similar winders, but usually with a clamp base, are produced in inexpensive wood and used today, but greater pleasure is afforded winding a hank of wool on an example such as this. The piece below is an English hand-winder in bakelite, used for yarns of shorter length and described as "The 'Gleam' Silk and Wool Winder ... Regd. No. 688276".

Above: German steel winder, c.1890, **£45–65/ $70–105**; right: English bakelite hand-winder, c.1940, **£5–10/ $8–16**

Glossary

Averys Ornate brass needle-cases, originally patented and made by William Avery, but also made by other makers of sewing accessories

Back stamp Stamp of a porcelain manufacturer found inside a thimble, often used for dating the piece

Bodkin A large needle without a pointed end, for threading ribbon, elastic or cord

Bog oak Semi-petrified wood found in Irish bog land

Cartouche A plain panel within a decorative pattern, inscribed with initials, date, etc

Chatelaine Accessories carried suspended from the waist by a clasp

Clamp A means of securing a tool to the table top

Damascene A design in silver and gold, chased on to blue steel

Dorcas A patented steel-cored thimble

Emery A cushion of grains of emery (corundum) used to remove rust and polish

Etui (pronounced et-wee) Small container of fitted tools

Finger guard A shield worn, usually on the index finger of the left hand, to protect against the point of a needle

Hemming bird A clamp that assisted in the sewing of a hem

Hussif A small cylindrical container of emergency sewing tools

Knitting sheath A tool used to hold a knitting needle firmly, allowing the knitter a third "hand"

Lucet A tool for making cord

Mauchline ware (pronounced mock-lin) Scottish wooden souvenir ware.

Mint In the original condition

Mother-of-pearl The smooth lustrous lining of calcium carbonate found in the shells of oysters, abalone and mussels

Nanny brooch A brooch containing emergency sewing supplies

Necessaire A container of fitted tools – larger than an etui but smaller than a needlework box

Needle prints Coloured prints by Baxter and Le Bond, affixed to needle boxes

Palais Royal Accessories of mother-of-pearl made in the vicinity of the Palace of Versailles, France

Piercy's Patent A process of fusing tortoiseshell with metals such as silver or steel

Pin ball A small finely knitted circular pincushion, decorated with letters or numbers, suspended by a cord

Pin money A term derived from the process of calculating the Victorian household's budget for purchasing pins; it also refers to pins given in lieu of small change

Pin wheel A flat circular holder for pins

Sampler A piece of embroidery demonstrating needle skills, often created over a number of years

Scissor sheath A safety cover for the blades of scissors

Shagreen Fish skin that has been dyed green

Spool knave A free-flowing thread supplier, which was hung from the waist

Stanhope "peep" A miniature lens and photograph positioned at the end of a sewing accessory

Stickware Tunbridge ware in a mosaic technique

Stiletto Pointed tool for creating design holes in fabric

Sweetgrass Straw accessories made by Native Americans

Veneer A thin layer of wood laid over an inexpensive wooden core as decoration

Tailor's thimble An indented ring that pushed the needle using the side of one's finger

Tambour hook A tool resembling a fine crochet hook, used to create embroidery from the reverse side of the fabric

Tatting shuttle A tool used to create tatting – a technique similar to crochet in appearance

Thimble Full A spirit (alcohol) measure in the shape of a large thimble

Thread winder A flat, variously shaped disc for storing thread

Tunbridge ware Wooden souvenir ware made in Kent

Vegetable ivory A material made from the corozo nut; the coquilla nut is also sometimes mistakenly called vegetable ivory

Waxer A container holding wax through which thread was passed to make it slippery

Yard rule A wooden measuring tool, used in the early 19thC, which was kept in the town's guildhall to formally check measurements

What to read

GENERAL REFERENCE

Andere, Mary
Old Needlework Boxes and Tools
(David & Charles, Newton Abbot, UK, 1971)

Groves, Sylvia
The History of Needlework Tools & Accessories
(Country Life Books, The Hamlyn Publishing Group, UK, 1966)

Holmes, Edwin F.
A History of Thimbles
(Cornwall Books, Rosemount, UK, 1985)

Holmes, Edwin F.
Thimbles (Gill & Macmillan Ltd, UK, 1976)

Johnson, Eleanor
Needlework and Embroidery Tools (Shire, UK, 1978, revised 1999)

McConnel, Bridget
The Story of Antique Needlework Tools
(Schiffer, USA, 1999)

McConnel, Bridget
The Story of the Thimble
(Schiffer, USA, 1997)

Proctor, Molly
Needlework Tools and Accessories – A Collector's Guide
(Batsford, UK, 1990)

Rainwater, Dorothy & Frank, Beryl
Silver Curios in the Home
(Schiffer, USA, 1999)

Rogers, Gay Ann
An Illustrated History of Needlework Tools and Accessories
(John Murray, USA, 1983)

Taunton, Nerylla
Antique Needlework Tools & Embroideries
(The Antique Collectors' Club, UK, 1997)

Whiting, Gertrude
Old Time Tools and Toys of Needlework
(Columbia University Press, USA, 1928 & Dover Publications Inc NY, USA, 1971)

SPECIALIST BOOKS

Baker, John
Mauchline Ware
(Shire, UK, 1985)

Cummins, Genivieve & Taunton, Nerylla
Chatelaines – Utility to Glorious Extravagance
(The Antique Collectors' Club, UK, 1994)

Gill, Margaret A.V.
Tunbridge Ware (Shire, UK, 1985)

Horowitz, Estelle & Mann, Ruth
Victorian Brass Needlecases
(Needlework Treasures, USA, 1990)

McGowan, Susan
Thimbles of Australia
(Kangaroo Press PTY, Australia, 1998)

Rogers, Gay Ann
American Silver Thimbles
(Haggerston Press, USA, 1989)

Von Furstenburg, Princess Ira
Tartan Ware
(Pavilion Books Ltd, UK, 1996)

Where to buy & see

It is best to buy from a specialist dealer to ensure the condition and cost of chosen purchases, but do not hesitate to buy a bargain anywhere when you spot one. If it is something you do not need for your own collection you can part-exchange it with a dealer and trade it in for that elusive piece you have always wanted!

SPECIALIST DEALERS

Pat Budd
Sussex, UK
Tel: 01935 884401
(Fridays to Sundays only)

Sonia Cordell
Suffolk, UK
Tel: 01394 282254
(Sales list)

Trixie Frampton
Dorset, UK
Tel: 01935 891395

Bunny Gorfinkle
Massachusetts, USA
Tel: (001) 781 631 6109

Fern Larking Keo
Ohio, USA
Tel: (001) 419 352928

Carolyn Meacham
Virginia, USA
Tel: (001) 804 794 8648

Inez Oaktree
Vlaardingen, Netherlands
Tel: (0031) 104 746715

Jennie Patterson
Gloucester, UK
Tel: 01452 812620

Deborah Silvestro
New York, USA
Tel: (001) 914 331 3120

Kay Sullivan
AB Amstelveen
Netherlands
Tel: (0031) 206 431954
(Sales list)

Marcie Thueringer
Washington, USA
Tel: (001) 425 486 0444

Elizabeth Wackiorski
London, UK
Tel: 020 7221 0353
(Stall at Portobello,
Saturdays only)

Joyce Williams
California, USA
Tel: (001) 916 967 1671

SOCIETIES & GROUPS
United Kingdom:
Dorset Thimble Society
Mrs Joan Mee (Secretary)
8 St Michael's Road,
Bournemouth,
Dorset BH22 0EG
(3 magazines, 3 meetings a
year, International Conference
alternate years)

Mauchline Collectors Club
Unit 37
Romsey Industrial Estate
Greatbridge Road
Romsey, Hants SO51 0HR
(Newsletter and meetings)

Thimble Society (Commercial)
179 Malden Road
London NW5 4HT
(Postal address only; colour
sales catalogue, annual
meetings, stall at Portobello –
Saturdays only)

Welsh Thimblers
c/o Denise Jenkins
1 Penprysg Road, Pencoed
Bridgend, Mid Glamorgan,
South Wales CF35 6SS

USA:
Thimbletter II
Mrs Dorthy Griffith (Editor)
4316 Hale Drive SW
Lilburn, Georgia
30057-4114, USA
(Newsletter alternate months)

**Thimble Collectors
International**
Mrs Kay Connors
(Membership Chairman)
2594E Upper Hayden Lake Road

Hayden Lake, Indiana
83835-9084, USA
(News bulletin and inter-
national convention alternate
years; contact with local groups)

Australia:
Needlework Tool Collectors
Society of Australia
c/o Helen Cunningham
13 Brixton Rise
Glen Iris, Victoria 3146
(Monthly meetings Feb–Dec)

Digitabulists Society
Jack Turner (Chairman)
23 Harrow Road
Somerton Park 5044
South Australia

Germany:
Freunde des Fingerhut E.V.
c/o Judith Jungbludt,
Kohlesmuehle 6, 97993
Creglingen
(Newsletter, 2 meetings a year)

Indonesia:
Jakarta Thimble Group
c/o Natalie Sutadisastra
JL Tedet Timur IV/21, Jakarta-
Selatan 12820, Jakarta

Israel:
Kibbutz Yizreel
c/o Aliza Factor
D.N. Yizreel 19350

Netherlands:
The Dutch Thimble
Association (Commercial)
Kleine Overstraat 37
7411 JH Deventer
(Sales catalogue and meetings)

South Africa:
South African Thimble
Society
Jenny Scharff (Chairman)
PO Box 74439
Turffontein 2140
(Newsletter, 4 meetings a year)

MUSEUMS
If you wish to see items of
particular interest, write or
telephone the museum at
least four weeks before your
intended visit. Usually, this
enables you to view items not
currently on public display.

United Kingdom:
Bethnal Green
Museum of Childhood
Cambridge Heath Road
London E2 9PA
Tel: 020 8983 5203

Birmingham Museum
& Art Gallery
Chamberlain Square
Birmingham B3 3DH
Tel: 0121 2352834

The British Museum
Great Russell Street
London WC1B 3DG
Tel: 020 7636 1555

Castle Museum
Eye of York
York YO1 1RY
Tel: 01904 653611

Kay Shuttleworth Collection
Gawsthorp Hall, Padiham
Nr. Burnley BB12 8UA
Tel: 01282 778511

Killerton House
Broadclyst
Exeter EX5 3LE
Tel: 01392 881345

Museum of Childhood
42 High Street
Edinburgh EH1 1TG
Tel: 0131 529 4142

Museum of Costume
4, The Circus
Bath BA1 2EW
Tel: 01225 477752

The Museum of London
150 London Wall
London, EC2Y 5HN
Tel: 020 7600 3699

Museum of Welsh Life
St Fagan's
Cardiff CF5 6XB
Tel: 029 2056944

Salisbury & Wiltshire
Museum
The Kings House
65 The Close
Salisbury SP1 2EN
Tel: 01722 332151

Science Museum
Exhibition Road
South Kensington
London SW7 2DP
Tel: 020 7938 8000

Ulster Folk & Transport
Museum
Cultra, Holywood
Co. Down
N. Ireland BT18 0EY
Tel: 01232 428428

Victoria & Albert Museum
Cromwell Road
London SW7
Tel: 020 7942 2209

Wallace Collection
Manchester Square
London W1
Tel: 020 7935 0687

USA:
The Colonial Williamsburg
Foundation
Williamsburg
VA 23185-1776
Tel: (001) 804 220 7508

Old Sturbridge Village
1 Old Sturbridge Village Road
Sturbridge MA 01566
Tel: (001) 508 347 3362

Smithsonian Institute
Textile Division
12th St & Constitution Ave NW
Washington DC 20560
Tel: (001) 202 357 1889

Australia:
The Embroiderers' Guild
76 Queen Street
Concord West, 2138 Sydney
Tel: (0061) 2 974 325 01

Belgium:
Gruuthumuseum-Dyver
17-8000 Bruges
Tel: (0032) 50 448762

Musées Royaux d'Art
et d'Histoire
Parc de Cinquantenaire 10
1000 Brussels
Tel: (0032) 2 534 2552

Canada:
Maryboro Lodge, Fenelon
Falls Museum
50 Oak Street
Fenelon Falls
Ontario KOM 1NO
Tel: (001) 705 887 1044

Royal British Columbia
Museum
675 Belleville Street
Victoria BC V8W 9W2
Tel: (001) 250 356 7226

Denmark:
Den Gamle By-Danmarks
Kobstadmuseum
Viborgvej 2
800 Arthus C
Tel: (0045) 8612 3188

Finland:
National Museum of Finland
Mannerheimintie 34
00100 Helsinki
Tel: (00358) 940501

France:
Musée du Louvre-
Palais du Louvre
107 Rue de Rivoli
75058 Paris
Tel: (0033) 0140 205317

Germany:
Fingerhutmuseum
D97993 Creglingen
Kohlesmuhle
Tel: (0049) 79 33 370

Schmuckmuseum
Jan Strasse, 42-D75173
Pforzheim
Tel: (0049) 7231 392126

Japan:
Mingeikan, Japan Folk
Craft Museum
3.33 Komaba Merguro Ku
Tokyo 153
Tel: (0081) 3 3467 4527

Netherlands:
Amsterdam Historisch
Museum
Kalverstraat 92
Nieuwezijds Voorburgwal 357
P.O. Box 3302
1001 AC Amsterdam
Tel: (0031) 20 523 1822

New Zealand:
Auckland Museum Te Papa
Whakahiku
Domain Drive
Auckland 1030
Tel: (0064) 9 309 0443

Russia:
The Hermitage
Dvortsovaya Nabierezhnaya
a Ulitsa Street
St Petersburg
Tel: (007) 812 110 3420

South Africa:
National Cultural
History Museum
189 Meer Street
Sunnyside
Pretoria 0132
Tel: (0027) 12 3411320

Spain:
Museo Arqueológico
Carrera del Darro 41
18010
Granada
Tel: (0034) 58 226279

Index

ACKNOWLEDGMENTS

All pictures photographed by Steve Tanner for Octopus Publishing Group Ltd, courtesy of Elaine Gaussen. The author would like to thank the following people for their help and support: Philip Gaussen, Elizabeth Wackiorski, Sylvia Norton, the editorial team at Miller's, Steve Tanner and Lucile Guilbert.